THE TIME OF HER LIFE

THE TIME OF HER LIFE LESLEY MCINTYRE

JONATHAN CAPE
LONDON

'The most important thing I learned on Tralfamadore was that when a person dies he only appears to die. He is still very much alive in the past, so it is very silly for people to cry at his funeral. All moments, past, present, and future, always have existed, always will exist. The Tralfamadorians can look at all the different moments just the way we look at a stretch of the Rocky Mountains, for instance. They can see how permanent all the moments are, and they can look at any moment that interests them. It is just an illusion we have here on Earth that one moment follows another one, like beads on a string, and that once a moment is gone it is gone forever.'

'When a Tralfamadorian sees a corpse, all he thinks is that the dead person is in a bad condition in that particular moment, but that the same person is just fine in plenty of other moments. Now, when I myself hear that somebody is dead, I simply shrug and say what the Tralfamadorians say about dead people, which is "So it goes". '

KURT VONNEGUT, *SLAUGHTERHOUSE 5*

INTRODUCTION

My daughter Molly was born at St Thomas' Hospital in London on 19 October 1984. Within the first few days of her life I was told that it was highly unlikely that she would survive more than a few weeks or months at the most and that in all probability she would never leave the hospital. A biopsy had revealed an abnormality in the formation of her muscles and the prognosis was very pessimistic. In spite of this I did take her home and she lived until 8 February 1999. In all of this time Molly's condition was never properly diagnosed.

Before her birth I assumed that I would be able to combine my career as a photographer with being a parent. I did achieve this but not in the manner I had anticipated. Commissions that I would have pursued had my child been more robust were not possible. I found myself grounded in our domestic life, the demands of such a fragile child being very particular. But I did not stop taking photographs. I carried a camera all the time and began recording the details of the day to day. I found observing childhood absolutely fascinating. These photographs are in chronological order and reveal the story of what actually happened to Molly over the fourteen years of her life.

This is a story that crosses all barriers of race, class and gender. Any family, at any time or anywhere can find themselves confronted by the reality of disability. I hope that by the time her disability becomes evident the viewer has already engaged with the person contained within such a delicate housing. The photographs reveal the whole human being, not just the part that is failing. The book is a portrait of a whole life virtually from birth until death. I bore witness to her life in the most intimate way. These photographs are the evidence.

Having spent so many years fighting so that my child would not be socially and educationally marginalised by her physical disability, I am fully aware of how resistant many people are to engaging with such subject matter. Their resistance is not confined to disability alone, but to death as well and especially to the most taboo form – child death. The irony is that I believe she had or *has* something to teach them. She was compassionate, intelligent and philosophical about her own limitations. In that sense she was a realist but in spite of all the obvious things that weighed against her she found a way of relishing her opportunities. In my opinion Molly was a privileged child. I brought her up understanding that fact. When I say privileged, I mean no amount of additional material wealth would have enhanced her quality of life significantly, unlike the majority of children on this planet. Molly's school had above the national average of free school meals, which is an obvious indicator of parental income, or rather lack of income, and she was aware of this.

Molly was a bright child attending mainstream schools at both primary and secondary levels where she always achieved a very high academic standard. She felt part of the broader society and was very much at home within it. In the last weeks of her life she said, 'I have a brain that works and a body that doesn't.' Even more significantly, six days before she died she said, 'I've been healthy all my life until now'. Miraculously she never saw herself as a *sick* child until the very end. I hope these photographs reveal the difference between having life (a pulse) and *living* a life.

After the initial prognosis every day we had together felt like a reprieve. Enabling Molly to have the quality of life she enjoyed meant my career was effectively put on hold. I dealt with a range of professionals throughout her fourteen years because she was someone who required cross-agency support. The practicalities surrounding the parenting of such a child are daunting. I would add that I separated from Molly's father when she was two and a half and consequently I was a single parent dealing with these issues. In her latter years I was a full-time carer. I always sensed that it would come to this and never doubted my desire to fulfil this role.

For myself, this book is about how to live with no guarantees. In other words it is about what everyone deals with but pretends that they don't. I believe that in spite of her frailty she lived her life with courage and surprising gusto at times and, almost more importantly, she died with great dignity at home surrounded by those who adored her. For all the agony of witnessing her physical deterioration, her vitality kept everyone going. If she was capable of hooting with laughter at Eddie Izzard in spite of her profound emaciation – then so could everyone else. She helped us through it. I was guided by her to the end. All the time I had a sense of what this child was capable of, which was a great deal, and even then she would confound my expectations and astonish me. In the last thirty-six hours of her life Molly got very shirty with the community paediatric nursing back-up. By then she was on a cocktail of medication, including anti-nausea drugs, and I remember her saying, 'Nobody told me what the side-effects of this medication were going to be.'

She did not like anything that made her drowsy. She was so articulate and lucid – mature beyond her years – and that was humbling to witness.

Molly got very angry with me one night a few days before she died. I was turning her to avoid bedsores and she was furious that she was dying. She was impatient with me. I felt desperate and remember saying, 'Darling, if there was anything I could do I would be doing it.' And very quietly she said, 'I know, Mum.' Then she said something which overwhelmed me, 'I'd love to be myself for just a little bit.' I knew what she meant. She just wanted to be well enough to re-engage with all the parts of her life she so relished. And just a few months prior to this moment she was still able to.

The book, although firmly fixed in one life story, could extend so far beyond it. Against all the odds she did live and loved so many people she encountered. I hope her legacy is that she gave those very people the capacity to engage with life and to *feel*.

An anecdote: Molly came home from her primary school one day and told me that a boy whom we knew was going to be excluded for difficult behaviour. Apparently the class was invited to discuss the issue. Molly told me she had spoken up on his behalf. She knew that his father had died very recently. She knew he was angry and very upset. Her argument was that if he was now rejected by the very people who knew him and who should be offering support, it would damage him further. She worried about how such rejection would affect him in the future. What belief would he have in other human beings? He was being threatened with isolation at the precise time he needed help and understanding. I found her reasoning breathtaking. The child remained in school. Whether Molly's input made any difference is irrelevant. What I do know is that she had a sense of possible long-term future damage.

Between birth and death you have living and dying. That's about it. It sounds so simple but we live in dreadful denial about the dying. I would love to demystify it a little without terrifying people. The end of a great life should be as celebratory as its beginning. Both stages are inevitably linked. It is how a human being engages with the middle bits that reflects who they really are – the journey they have travelled in their time – everything they have learned or not. It is a journey involving humility and a sense of your own insignificance, but also an awareness of what is possible even though it may be transient. Realism without pomposity.

It would be idiotic of me to deny that the book is a memorial to someone who taught me a daunting amount. Trying to put aside parental hubris, I hope her engagement with life is clearly reflected in this portrait. Together we lived in the present moment. It was not something we talked about – it was just how we lived day to day. Nobody knows for certain what the future holds. Nobody knows the exact moment they are going to die. There is no certainty. You just have to grasp and make the most of what you are given. As a friend of mine said soon after her death, 'Molly lived the life she got magnificently and I can't say that of many people.' The lessons are universal. If you are a human being who can bear to accept the reality that nothing is certain and life and death are inextricably linked – then I hope the work resonates for you.

LESLEY MCINTYRE

The hydrotherapy pool, St Thomas' Hospital, London, 1985

Molly in her father's arms, Tuscany, 1985

My mother, Molly and her Norwegian grandfather on holiday, Norway, 1986

Our flat, Oslo, 1986

I separated from Marius in July 1987. My mother came out to Norway
to help me with Molly on our return journey. We took a ferry from Oslo
to Harwich. I felt euphoric to be going home, whatever the future held.

My first New Year as a single parent was spent alone with Molly seriously
ill. I had her in my bed and intermittently she vomited up mucous – long,
stringy transparent mucous. I kept clearing her nose and throat – the
airways – pulling this mucous out. I was frightened she would be unable
to breathe. She had very poor respiratory function anyway. Her heartbeat
was racing and she was running a temperature. I realised she might die.
I cried and cried and felt overwhelmed. Then I remember looking down
at this dauntingly fragile, floppy baby and I suddenly understood that
whatever life she was going to have was entirely dependent on me. Every
decision from now on would be mine alone. I also knew that from that
moment on I lived with the inevitability of the unimaginable. My child
would die before me.

It sounds ludicrous but this realisation created a strange sense of calm.
I changed that night. I nursed Molly through that bout and many, many
more. I performed the function of an intravenous drip – spoon-feeding
her fluids twenty-four hours a day until the worst of the infection had run
its course. I knew I had to keep her hydrated otherwise we would end
up in hospital and for whatever reason I was determined that this would
not be the pattern of Molly's life – endless hospital admissions.

In retrospect I think that parenting Molly used every resource I had
developed as a human being, and others that I acquired through
knowing her.

The whole process inevitably was inextricably linked with my coming
to terms with her mortality.

My mother with Molly, Shortlands Farm, Pembrokeshire, Wales, 1987

On holiday, San Telmo, Majorca, 1988

Druidston Beach, Pembrokeshire, Wales, 1988

Esther and Molly, Brixton, London, 1989

At home, Brixton, London, 1989

On holiday, San Telmo, Majorca, 1989

The cafeteria, Brockwell Park, Lambeth, London, 1989

My mother with Molly, San Telmo, Majorca, 1989

Waiting to have her hair dried, Brixton, London, 1990

Spring Cottage, Pembrokeshire, Wales, 1990

The birthday present, Brixton, London, 1990

On holiday, just south of Rome, 1991

Hide and seek, Pembrokeshire, Wales, 1991

Esther, Molly, Anya and Helen at home, Brixton, London, 1991

Daisy and Molly in my parents' garden, Surrey, 1992

Exhibition of Veronica West's paintings, Nottingham, 1992

Borrowing a wheelchair, Sissinghurst, Sussex, 1992

My mother and Molly, the herb garden, Sissinghurst, Sussex, 1992

Deep Hollow Ranch, Montauk, Long Island, 1992

Indian Wells Beach, Amagansett, Long Island, 1992

Betty Hoeber's house, East Hampton, Long Island, 1992

At the hairdresser reading *Hello* magazine, London 1993

Hydrotherapy session, Thurlow Park School, Lambeth, London, 1993

Druidston Beach, Pembrokeshire, Wales, 1993

61

Bridesmaid at my brother's wedding, Hampshire, 1994

Esther and Molly dressing up, Brixton, London, 1994

Daisy and Molly dressing up, Saffron Walden, Essex, 1994

Molly in her bedroom, Brixton, London, 1995

She is that light one
Like the white from the window,
Reflected in our eyes,
And causing the shadow.

She bends like water,
Between our stone solid limbs,
A star round her neck,
Her voice a soft sighing ring.

I can remember,
She became more translucent,
Drifting away quietly,
To glitter in light's weaves and bends.

ROWEN HENZEL WEST
Written to mark the first anniversary of Molly's death

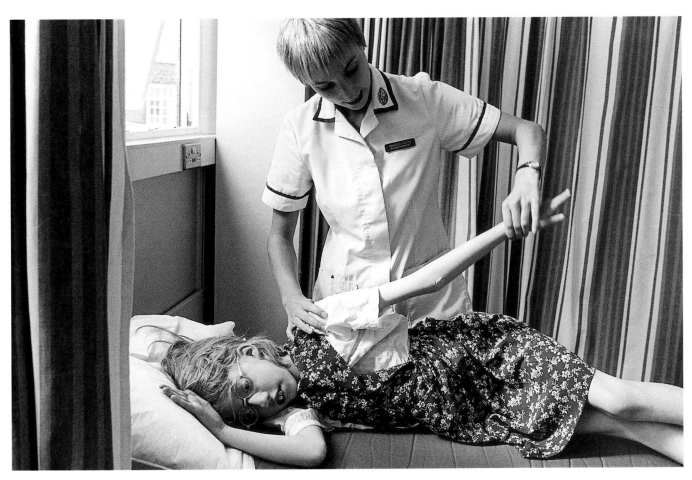

Physio assessment, Hammersmith Hospital, London, 1995

Red Nose Day, Sudbourne Primary School, Lambeth, London, 1995

The playground, Sudbourne Primary School, Lambeth, London, 1995

The Science Museum, New Jersey, 1995

Long Island, 1995

My parents' garden, Surrey, 1995

Molly, Pearl and Matay, Sudbourne School trip to The Croft, 1995

Molly photographing William on a Sudbourne School trip to The Croft, 1995

Demonstration against cuts in education, Piccadilly, London, 1995

Performance of Swan Lake, Covent Garden outreach programme, London, 1996

Brighton Pier, Sussex, 1996

Molly, Matay and Lanre on a Sudbourne School trip to Brighton, Sussex, 1996

<u>Timeline</u>

| 1984 | 1985 | 1986 | 1987 | 1988 | 1989 | 19 |

I was
born.
(oct 19th)

I started
at Montessori
School

I went to
live in Norway
for two years
with my mum
and my dad.

I got my
first kitten
and I called
her Grace.

Ⓐ
very detailed.

Grace had
five kittens

9.9.96

of my life

| | 1991 | 1992 | 1993 | 1994 | 1995 | 1996 |

I went on
my first trip
to America.

I started
at Elliott
school
(4th Sept)

broke
my leg
and I had
to go to
Great Ormond
Street Hospital.

My Granny
and Grandpa
had their
Golden
Anniversary.

I went back
to America
for the
seconds time.

Also my
Granny died

Finding a heated pool on holiday, Stackpole Centre, Pembrokeshire, Wales, 1996

Esther and Molly, Molly's thirteenth birthday party, Clapham, London, 1997

Auntie Carol and Princess Diana 14 . 9 . 97

Auntie Carol died of cancer on the 28th August
Princess Diana died in a car crash on the 31st August.

I was with my Mum in the car
When she got a message on her pager.
It told her to phone my Uncle's house at
                                    once.

Mum came out of the phone booth crying
She told me Carol had died.

I knew she was dying,
So, I was prepared
It was still very upsetting

I was with an old friend called Esther
When her younger sister came into our
                                        room
She told us Diana was dead
I could not believe it
I did'nt feel that upset though

Auntie Carol's service was a humanist
                            ceremony

Myself and my two little cousins, Angus
and Tommy were there.

We all laid bouquets around her coffin
The flowers we laid were very special
They were special because they were from
her own garden.

Princess Diana's service was a religious
service
Her sons flowers were not from her garden
Princess Diana's death
Seemed to be on T.V. the whole time for
days.

Auntie Carol left behind her two sons aged
3 and 5
And her husband, my Uncle Bruce.

Princess Diana left behind her two
sons aged 12 and 15
And her husband Prince Charles

Princess Diana's death,
It's just been a backdrop.

Daisy, Molly and her Uncle Bruce, Silchester, Hampshire. 1997

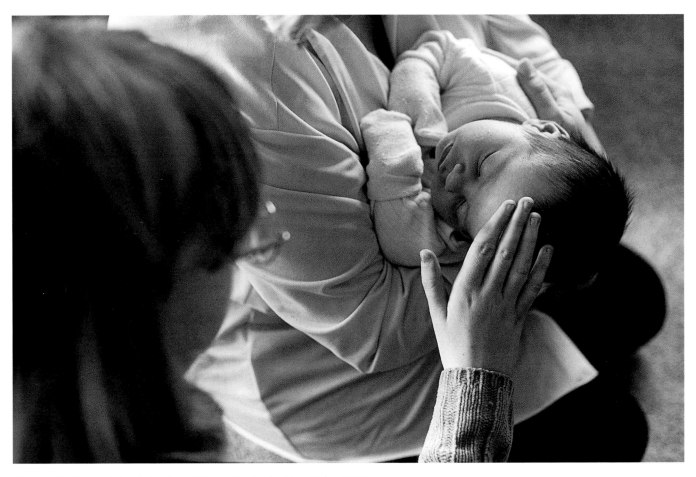

Meeting Beth's new baby, Luke, Broad Haven, Pembrokeshire, Wales, 1998

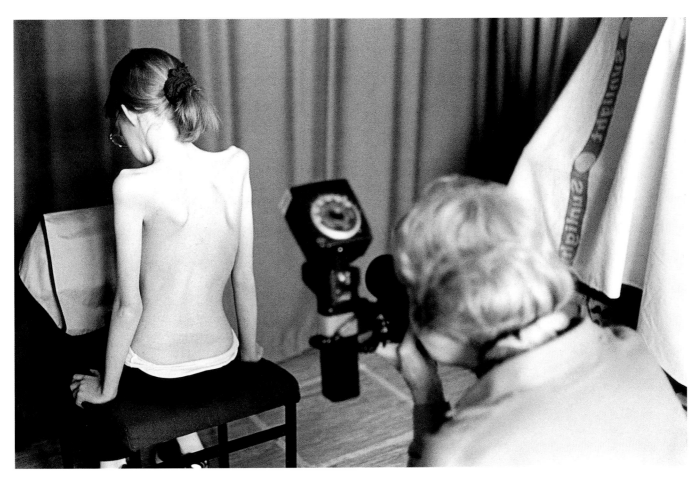

Medical photographer, Hammersmith Hospital, London, 1998

'I have a brain that works and a body that doesn't.'

Wine tasting, Moselle Valley, Germany, 1998

Year 8 Elliott Secondary School trip to the Rhine area, Germany, 1998

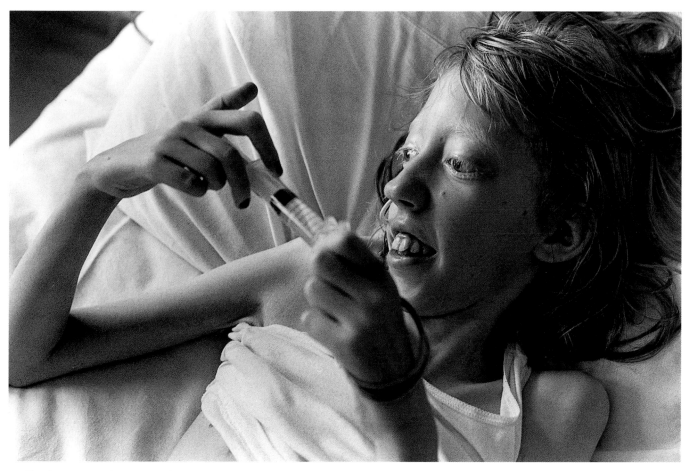

Molly administering her own medication, St Mary's Hospital, London, 1998

I long to have such a memorial of every being dear to me in the world.
It is not merely the likeness which is precious in such cases – but the
association and the sense of nearness involved in the thing … the fact
of the very shadow of the person lying there fixed forever! It is the very
sanctification of portraits I think – and it is not at all monstrous in me
to say, what my brothers cry out against so vehemently, that I would
rather have such a memorial of one I dearly loved, than the noblest
artist's work ever produced.

ELIZABETH BARRETT, FROM A LETTER
TO MARY RUSSELL MITFORD, 1843

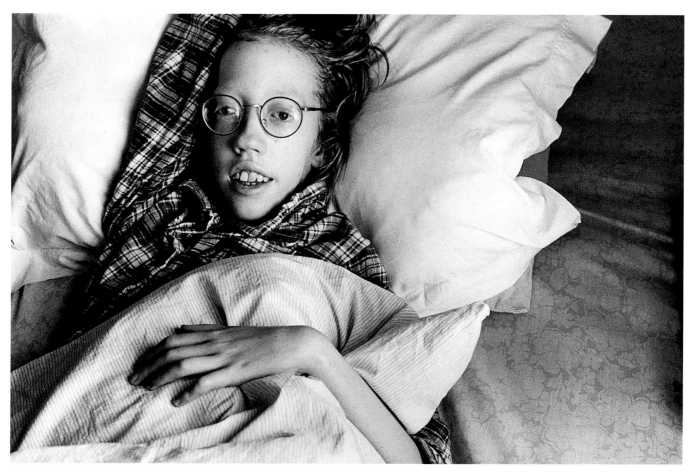

Molly at home four days before she died, Putney, London, 1999

I would particularly like to thank Dimitri Fanourakis for his invaluable advice and encouragement from the beginning and for his support throughout this project. I am very grateful to Mick Williamson, Head of Photography at the Sir John Cass Department of Art, Media and Design, London Metropolitan University for enabling me to print these pictures and for teaching me how to use multigrade paper. I must also thank Sarah Ainslie for her constant support and for recommending that I take the work to Mark Holborn at Jonathan Cape.

L. M.

Published by Jonathan Cape 2004

1 3 5 7 10 8 6 4 2

Photographs and introduction copyright Lesley McIntyre © 2004

Extract from *Slaughterhouse 5* by Kurt Vonnegut, published by Jonathan Cape.
Reprinted by kind permission of The Random House Group Ltd.

Poem, p.70, © Rowen Henzel West

First published in 2004 by Jonathan Cape, Random House,
20 Vauxhall Bridge Road, London SW1V 2SA

The Random House Group Limited Reg. No.954009

www.randomhouse.co.uk

A CIP catalogue for this book is available from the British Library

ISBN 0-224-072544

Designed by Mark Holborn and Antigone Konstantinidou

Printed in China by C & C Offset Printing Co.Ltd